THE VALUES TAUGHT BY THE SOLAR SYSTEM

THE MORAL VALUES ONE CAN LEARN FROM THE SOLAR SYSTEM

M. AISHWARYA JATHISH

Dedicated to the writing potential in me......................

Contents

Foreword

This book talks about the values one can learn from the solar system. The solar system is vast and beautiful but the values they provide us in even more greater. However we fail to notice the values provided by them.This book has been written to show the readers the values that the solar system provides us.

Preface

This book is about the values one can learn from the solar system. There are many things around us which we do not examine carefully and which we take for granted. We never consider solar system to be a teacher in our lives-a teacher who provides moral values to us, but yes , the solar system does teach us many values .We are going to look into these values in this book.

Acknowledgements

I thank Notion Press for being my publisher and also my family members for their support by which I could write this book. I thank my teachers and my friends as well for their huge support.

Prologue

Looking upon, solar system ,which we take for granted, as a teacher who teaches us moral values and ethics in our lives is difficult ,but, when we think that way, we come to understand the important values the solar system provides us, in our day-to-day live. This book has been written with the purpose of making the readers aware of the values provided by the solar system.

CHAPTER ONE

INTRODUCTION

The solar system is something we never look upon in this manner.I know that very well.The reason is because, we take it for granted. When we take things for granted, we fail to think deeply about them.When we think deeply about the solar system and its working, we come across the values they provide us, which are very useful in our day-to-day lives.

Many values are provided by the solar system which we fail to notice. Once we come across them, we come to know the importance of solar-system in our lives-not as a matter of science or astronomy, but as a teacher who teaches us ethics and moral values, which would help us live our lives happily.

This book is written with the purpose of making the readers aware of the moral values provided by the solar system in our everyday lives.

CHAPTER TWO

UNITY IN DIVERSITY

Each planet in the solar system is different from one another. Some are small, some big, some are blazing hot and some are freezing cold. Yet all of them have the same goal-orbitting the sun, which they do together, in their own respective orbits, without affecting the movement of one another.

This beautiful way of working of the solar system symbolizes unity in diversity. It is one of the important value taught by the solar system in our everyday lives.If we too work like the planets in the solar system, following the principle of unity in diversity and stop all the violence and crimes in the society, we could make the world a more better place to live.

SATURN'S RINGS

Saturn is known for having many rings around it. Despite having those rings around it, the planet continues orbitting around the sun, at a fixed pace.

Saturn's rings represents the opposition and the pressure which surrounds us like how the rings surround Saturn. However, as shown by the planet, one must always move forward in life without letting the world stop our progress.

CHAPTER FOUR

DECEPTIVE APPEARANCE

The stars look small to us when looked from the Earth, but in reality, they are even bigger than the Sun.

Likewise, outward appearances can be deceptive. We must judge one, not by the outward appearance, but by their behaviour. We must try to gather information about them before judging them at the very first time.

The stars provide a good example in this case .

CHAPTER FIVE

THE BIG BANG THEORY-STARTING FROM A SPOT

The whole universe started from a small spot, according to the Big Bang Theory. Likewise, great people are those who come from nothing and reach high levels in their lives.

Therefore, we must also aim to acheive something big in our lives, irrespective of our present status.This is what the Big Bang Theory teach us.

CHAPTER SIX

LEARNING FROM PLUTO

We can learn from the dwarf -planet, Pluto. Pluto shares its orbit with four more dwarf planets,namely-Eris, Haumea, Ceres and Makemake.

Like Pluto, we too must share our accessories with others and do good deeds such as helping the poor, donnating for a good-cause etc.

DARK ENERGY AND DARK MATTER

Though the space looks dark, in it is the Dark Energy and Dark Matter which is blind to naked eyes.

Likewise, we have hidden-talents inside us, which we need to identify, bring out and use it appropriately.

This example of Dark Energy and Dark Matter in space, motivates us to bring out our hidden talents and helps us concentrate on our inner-self.

CHAPTER EIGHT

BLACK HOLES AND THE DANGERS

Black holes are there in the space, as big dangers to the objects, people and animals who go to space or which travels in the space. They pull the object towards them and then, once the object goes inside it, it would never come out.

Likewise, dangers are there in every step we take, to pull us down, just like how the black holes pulls objects towards it.

We must protect ourselves from the dangers of our everyday lives.

CHAPTER NINE

THE JOY OF GIVING

The sun is thought to be powerful because it provides with heat and light. Likewise, one can be more powerful and happy, only by donating things to others.

Our power or true strength lies in donation, not in our selfish-acts or behaviours. Therefore, we must also provide things to others in order to live happily and be considered powerful in the society.

We must remember that there is no happiness bigger than the one that lies in JOY OF GIVING.

Conclusion

These are the values which the solar-system provides us and that one expects to have in his or her life.

These values make us lead our lives happily, helps us in achieving great things and ....

Above all, makes this world-A BETTER PACE TO LIVE IN!!!